EDUCATION FOR EVERYONE SERIES

Creatures And Plants In Florida

by Jacqueline Gonzalez

ISBN-10: 1466440333
ISBN-13: 978-1466440333

Table of Contents

Amphibians - Frogs & Toads

Green Tree Frog

- Found on window sills of houses or buildings at night, looking for insects to eat
- Croaks more when the air is humid before it rains

Frogs have smooth skin while toads have bumpy skin.

POISONOUS

Cane Toad (also called Marine Toad, Giant Toad)

- Brought into Florida in 1955 to eat white grubs that were destroying the sugar canes
- Eats ants, beetles, even dog or cat food

1

Animals

Nine Banded Armadillo

- It cannot roll itself into a ball like the three banded armadillo can.
- If captured, it plays dead. If this doesn't work, it starts kicking.
- Known to carry the leprosy disease

Evening Bat

- Can eat over 3000 insects in one night
- Because of its poor eyesight, it uses echolocation to locate and identify objects. It emits a sound and then determines how long before it hears the sound's echo. The shorter the time, the closer it is to its target. Dolphins also use this method.

Florida Black Bear

- Can climb a 100 foot tree in 30 seconds
- Can smell food from a mile away
- Hibernates for 3 to 5 months, starting in October or November
- Can weigh up to 450 pounds

Animals

Bobcat

- The size of a medium dog
- Stays away from people and lives most of its life alone
- Eats rabbits and rats
- Spends most of its time moving around, especially during sunrise and sunset

White Tailed Deer

- When it senses danger, it holds its tail up, showing the white part of the tail.
- The hooves are the toenails of the third and fourth toes of each foot.
- Has 4 connected stomachs like cows
- Can see blue and yellow but not red
- Deer ticks, which carry Lyme Disease, are found on deer.

Red Fox

- The size of a small dog
- Lives in an underground burrow
- Lives in meadows and fields, whereas the gray fox lives in forests
- Hunts by springing into the air and then pinning its prey with its front feet

Animals

Eastern Mole

- Is 6½ to 7½ inches long
- Spends most of its time underground. As it digs, it pushes the dirt to the surface, resulting in a mole hill.
- Its eyes and ears are covered by skin and fur so it cannot see except for whether it is light or dark outside. It can, however, hear very well.

Nutria

- Brought to Florida in 1955 from fur farms in South America
- Most prevalent in the Tampa Bay area
- Eats by tearing out the grass by the roots
- Is 14 inches long, not including the tail

Opossum

- Commonly called "possum"
- Has 50 teeth, more than any other North American animal
- People say "playing possum" because in times of extreme fear, the opossum goes into a near coma (deep sleep) for up to 4 hours.

Animals

Otter

- Spends most of its day grooming
- Can dive up to 60 feet below the water surface
- Is a social animal that makes several noises such as whistles, growls, snarls, chuckles, and high pitched screams

Marsh Rabbit

- Rabbits produce 2 kinds of poop. One is hard fecal pellets and the other is soft cecal pellets which are packed full of vitamins and nutrients that the rabbit needs. So, once a day or so the rabbit poops the cecal pellets and then eats them.

Raccoon

- Eats just about anything: fruits, nuts, acorns, vegetables, seeds, insects, eggs, fish, frogs, crayfish, small mammals, pet food, and garbage
- Can open coolers and garbage cans
- Usually lives in a hollow tree
- When the babies are scared, they cover their eyes with their hands.
- Known for carrying the rabies disease

Animals

Cotton Rat

- Is about 12 inches long, including the tail
- Molars are s-shaped if you look at them from above
- Was used to study polio and typhus disease in the 1930's and cystic fibrosis disease in 1984

Striped Skunk

- Eats mostly insects
- When threatened, it sprays a bad smelling liquid out of its anus. It can spray as far as 15 feet to reach its target. The glands hold enough liquid to spray 5 to 6 times.
- Known for carrying the rabies disease which affects the nervous system

Eastern Gray Squirrel

- Lives in tree holes or in nests made of leaves
- If suddenly disturbed, it will make a barking noise.
- Eats acorns, nuts, fruits, berries, bird eggs, and sometimes insects
- Known for collecting and storing food. It will collect as many nuts as it can fit in its cheek pouches. It then buries the nuts in various locations. Later on, it uses its memory and smell to find the buried nuts.

Birds

Red-Winged Blackbird

- Found in marshes and fields

Cardinal

- Tends to attack its reflection in a window

Grackle

- Found in large flocks sitting on lawns, crops or telephone lines

Birds migrate over thousands of miles to the same places each year. They can do this because they have a chemical in their eye that allows them to see magnetic field lines. They also have magnetic crystals in their beaks that create a magnetic map for them to follow.

Great Horned Owl

- Claws are stronger than a German Shepherd dog's bite.

Northern Mockingbird

- Perches on telephone poles, street lights

Red-Bellied Woodpecker

- Noisy bird with many different calls

Birds

Brown Pelican

- Dives for fish from above and catches them in its bill. Then it tips its bill back to drain out the water and swallow the fish.

Egret

- Symbol of the National Audubon Society
- Many egrets were killed in the late 1800's so their feathers could be used to decorate hats.

Great White Heron

- Eats fish and mice
- Sometimes chokes by trying to swallow fish that are too big
- Flies 20 to 30 miles per hour

Ibis

- Lives in large flocks and migrates in a "V" pattern
- Uses its beak to probe just beneath the water or ground surface to get insects or crayfish to eat

Birds

Osprey

- Has a wingspan of 5 to 6 feet
- Diet consists of fish
- Will fly 50 to 100 feet above the water
- Closes its nostrils before it dives into the water
- Only the osprey and the owl have an outer toe that they can rotate. This allows them to have two toes in front and two toes in back. This is quite helpful in holding on to their food.
- Sometimes eagles steal the osprey's food in midair.

Sandhill Crane

- Sometimes found walking in neighborhoods
- Can bite you
- All throughout the year it dances, runs, and leaps high in the air.

Snake Bird (Anhinga)

- Called Snake Bird because when it swims, it looks like a snake swimming with its head up high out of the water
- Since its feathers are not waterproof, it can be seen with its wings spread out to dry.

Fish - Freshwater

Black Crappie

- Also known as speckled perch
- Found offshore in lakes or in large, slow-moving, clear water rivers
- A big catch is 14 inches
- Best bait: minnows, grass shrimp

Bluegill

- Likes shallow water in lakes and ponds
- A big catch is 11 inches
- Best Bait: crickets, live worms

Largemouth Bass

- Found in lakes and rivers
- Found in shallow water in the morning and then in deeper water as the sun rises
- A big catch is 24 inches
- Best Bait: golden shiners, plastic worms

Striped Bass

- Found in the cooler rivers in Northern Florida
- A big catch is 30 inches
- Best Bait: live shad, lures

Fish - Freshwater

Channel Catfish

- Bottom feeder found in rivers
- Most active before the sun sets and at night
- A big catch is 31 inches
- Best Bait: chicken liver, shrimp

Spotted Sunfish

- Found in slow-moving streams and rivers with sand or gravel bottoms
- Feeds on the bottom but also rises to the surface to feed
- A big catch is 8 inches
- Best Bait: live worms, crickets

Blue Tilapia

- Found in lakes, ponds, rivers, streams, and canals
- A big catch is 18 inches
- Best Bait: hot dogs, bread balls, dog food, or live worms

11

Fish - Saltwater

Crevalle Jack

- Found near the shore and in the open sea
- State Record is 57 pounds
- Eats small fish

Dolphin Fish (Mahi-Mahi)

- Found in the open ocean
- State Record is 81 pounds
- Eats squid, fish

Flounder

- Found near shore on sandy or mud bottoms
- State Record is over 20 pounds
- Eats shrimp, crabs, fish

Goliath Grouper

- Found around docks, in deep holes, on ledges, and around oyster banks
- State Record is 680 pounds
- Eats shrimp, crabs, fish

Striped Mullet

- Found near shore
- Not eligible for a state record
- Eats algae, tiny marine animals

Pompano

- Found along sandy beaches, oyster banks, and over grass beds
- State Record is over 8 pounds
- Eats crabs, live shrimp

Fish - Saltwater

Red Snapper

- Found on sandy or mud bottoms
- State Record is over 46 pounds
- Eats small fish, crabs, shrimp

Sailfish

- Found near the Gulfstream (a warm Atlantic ocean current) in waters 600 feet deep
- State Record is 126 pounds
- Eats fish, squid

Snook

- Found in warm water near shore along mangroves, seawalls, bridges, and pilings
- State Record is just over 44 pounds
- Eats live pinfish, mullet, shrimp

Spanish Mackerel

- Found near shore and in the ocean
- Likes warm waters
- State Record is 12 pounds
- Eats small fish, squid

Sheepshead

- Found around seawalls, oyster banks, and in tidal creeks
- State Record is just over 15 pounds
- Eats live shrimp, fiddler crabs

Tarpon

- Found near shore around salt marshes and mangroves
- State Record is 243 pounds
- Eats live shrimp, pinfish

Insects - Ants

Stinging Ant: Fire Ant

- Very aggressive if you disturb it
- Stepping on its mound will cause hundreds of ants to come out, crawl up your leg, and attempt to sting you.
- Has a painful, burning sting which results in severe itching and a bump resembling a pimple

Fire Ant Bites

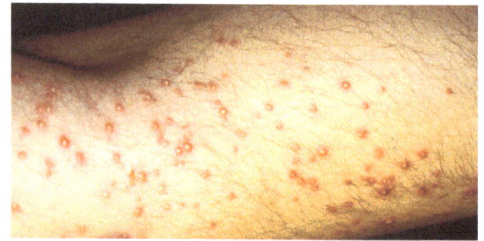

Fire Ant Mound
Irregular in Shape

Non-Fire Ant Mound
Regular in Shape

Non-Stinging Ant

- Several species of ants reside in Florida such as the white footed ant, ghost ant, crazy ant, pharaoh ant, acrobat ant, carpenter ant, and others.
- Although a couple of species may bite, they do not sting.

Insects - Bugs

Earwig

- Eats plants & insects
- Can be found in damp areas such as bathrooms
- Mother constantly washes her eggs
- If the mother dies, her children will eat her.

Firefly (Lightning Bug)

- Is actually a beetle
- Mostly found in Northern Florida
- When the firefly inhales, the oxygen combines with a substance called luciferin in the abdomen. This causes the abdomen to glow.

Cicada

- Lives 2 to 5 years
- Produces clicking sounds by tightening and loosening its muscles
- Sucks juice from tree roots
- Deep fried and eaten in Northern China

Katydid

- 2 inches long
- Eats leaves & flowers
- Rubs its front wings together to make sounds

Insects do not have oxygen-carrying red blood cells so their blood is clear, orange, yellow, or green.

Love Bug

- Came to Florida from Louisiana and Mississippi in 1947
- Doesn't bite
- Feeds on plant nectar
- Nuisance to motorists because it swarms. It appears twice a year: May & September. Its peak activity is at 10 am and it stops flying after sundown.

15

Insects - Bugs

Mole Cricket

- Lives for 1 to 2 years, like most insects
- 1 inch long
- Feeds on worms & roots
- Damages lawns & crops

Silverfish

- Lives 2 to 8 years
- ½ to ¾ of an inch long
- Likes moist areas like bathrooms
- Eats glue, book bindings, paper, and flour
- Can survive a year without eating

May or June Beetle

- Its eggs hatch into larvae called white grubs which do a lot of damage to lawns, crops & trees.

Stink Bug

- Can be green or brown
- ½ of an inch long
- Sucks plant juices and damages fruits
- Releases a smell that stinks

Praying Mantis

- Eats other insects
- Largest was 18 inches in China in 1929
- Is the only insect in the animal kingdom that has only one ear
- Known to sometimes eat the male

Walking Stick

- Feeds on leaves
- 1½ to 2½ inches long
- Sprays a painful milky liquid when threatened

16

Insects - Caterpillars & Butterflies

Black Swallowtail Caterpillar & Butterfly

Turns Into

Cloudless Sulphur Caterpillar & Butterfly

Turns Into

Gulf Fritillary Caterpillar & Butterfly

Turns Into

The color of butterflies is created by tiny scales on their wings.
Butterflies can live from a week to almost a year,
depending on the species.

17

Insects - Dragonflies & Butterflies

Dragonfly

- Eats mosquitoes
- Found around bodies of water
- Like all insects, it breathes through small holes in its abdomen called spiracles.

Monarch Caterpillar & Butterfly

 **Turns Into**

Some species, such as the Monarch, migrate from Mexico to Southern Canada, a distance of up to 3000 miles.

Zebra Longwing Caterpillar & Butterfly

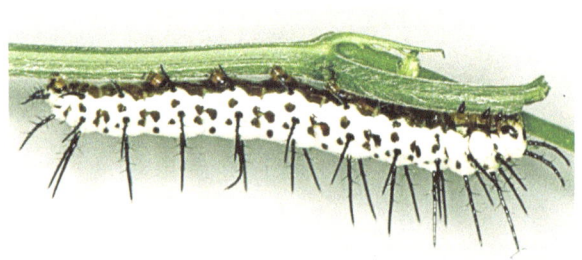 **Turns Into**

Insects - Caterpillars & Moths

Inside A Caterpillar: A Very Simple View

Insects, scorpions, spiders, crabs, shrimp, and lobster have this same setup of heart, digestive system, and nerve cord.

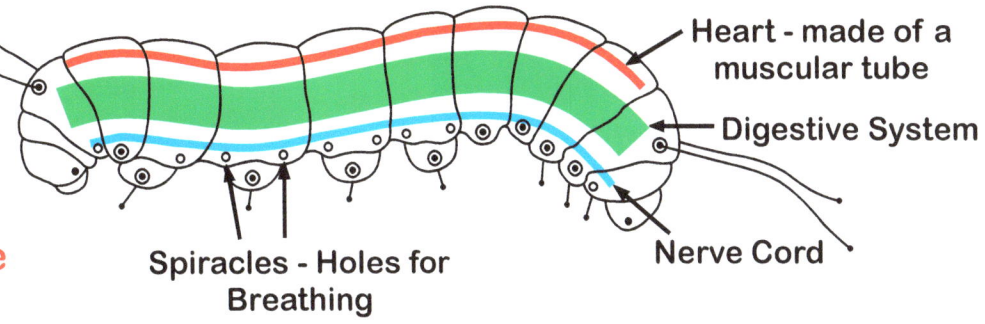

Heart - made of a muscular tube

Digestive System

Nerve Cord

Spiracles - Holes for Breathing

Saddleback Caterpillar & Moth

POISONOUS

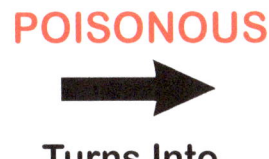

Turns Into

Puss Caterpillar & Moth

POISONOUS

Turns Into

Io Caterpillar & Moth

POISONOUS

Turns Into

19

Insects - Caterpillars & Moths

Fall Armyworm & Moth
- Eats grass & vegetable crops
- Creates a lot of damage

Turns Into

Banded Sphinx Caterpillar & Moth
- The moth is about 3 inches long.
- Likes evening primrose plants

Turns Into

Oleander Caterpillar & Polka Dot Wasp Moth
- The caterpillar is usually called the oleander caterpillar because it eats oleander leaves.

Turns Into

Insects - Cockroaches

<u>Cockroaches</u>
- Can run 3 miles per hour
- Can live a month without their head
- Can hold their breath for 40 minutes
- Do not like temperatures below 77 degrees Fahrenheit

German Cockroach

- ½ of an inch long
- Most common inside homes
- Hardest to get rid of because it reproduces so fast
- Eats table scraps, pet food, and book bindings

Egg Case Coming Out of Cockroach

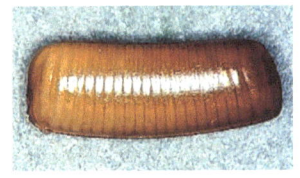

German Cockroach Egg Casing

Contains 30 to 40 eggs

Cockroaches are most active during the first 4 hours after lights out in the house.

Cockroaches leave chemical trails in their feces that tells other cockroaches where to go to find food. They like dark moist places and feed on sweets, cardboard, book bindings, and dead insects.

21

Insects - Cockroaches

American Cockroach

- 1½ inches long
- Also known as the Palmetto Bug
- Can be found outside or inside homes
- Eats sweets, book bindings, soiled clothing, soap, and grease
- Found in sewers, restaurants, and bakeries

Young American Cockroaches

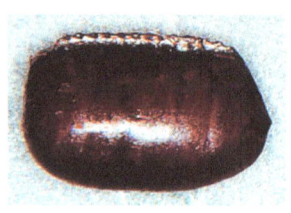

American Cockroach Egg Casing:
Contains 16 eggs

An adult female that is carrying eggs has orange blood.
The orange color is from a Vitamin A-like substance.
All other cockroach blood is colorless.

Australian Cockroach

- 1 inch long
- Lives around the outside of the house in leaves, shrubs, wood piles, and garages

Insects - Mosquitoes, Sandflies

Gnat

- Breeds in decaying vegetation
- Does not bite
- Males assemble in large swarms
- Comes out at dusk

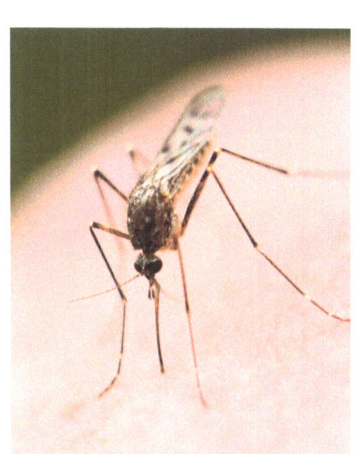

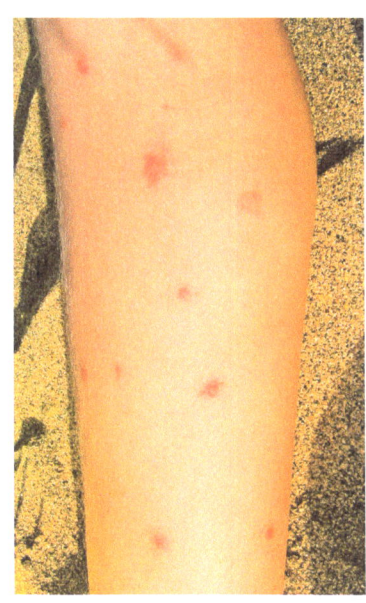

Mosquito Bites

Mosquito

- Adults live up to 2 weeks in nature.
- The male feeds on nectar & plant juices but the female needs a blood meal for her nutrition.
- Can transmit disease without getting sick themselves
- Attracted to people based on the carbon dioxide and octenol alcohol in their sweat. Octenol is formed during the breakdown of linoleic acid which is found in the foods we eat.

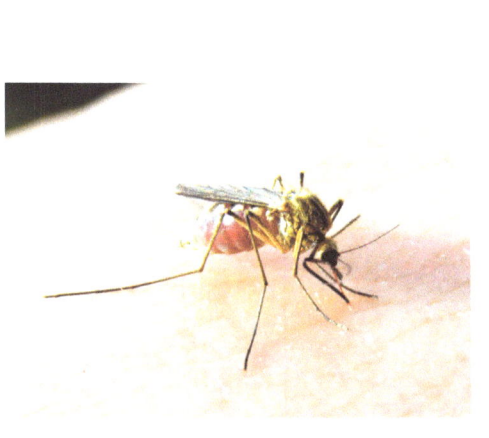

Sandfly (No-See-Um)

- Less than 1/8 of an inch long
- Abundant near the coast
- Only the female bites & takes blood
- Has small cutting teeth

Insects - Termites, Wasps

Termite (with wings)

Termite (without wings)

- Can be white, tan or black
- Can have wings or no wings
- Eats cellulose which is found in wood, paper, books, furniture, and cloth

Difference Between Termite and Ant

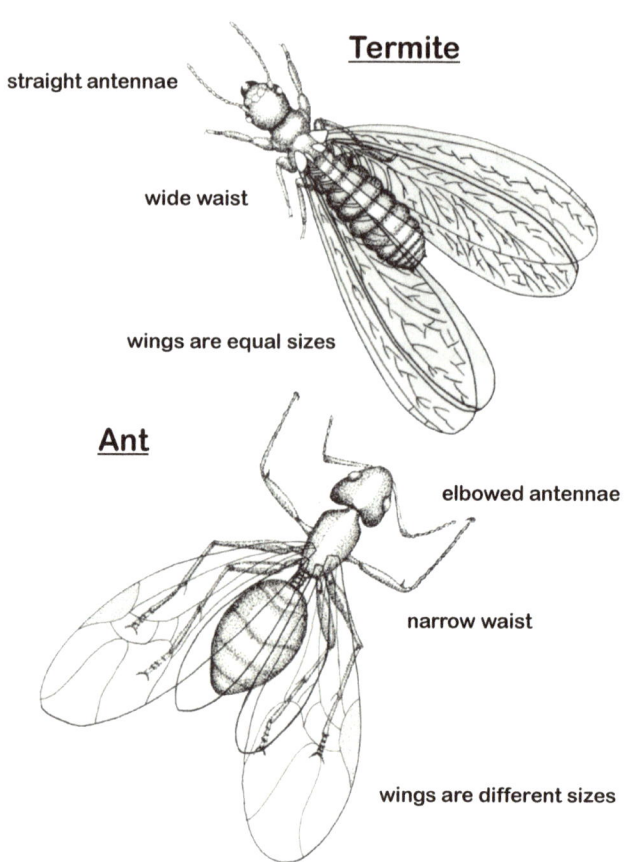

Termite

straight antennae

wide waist

wings are equal sizes

Ant

elbowed antennae

narrow waist

wings are different sizes

Termite wings fall off easily, ant wings don't.

Paper Wasp

- Is aggressive and will sting

Mud Dauber Wasp

- Is not aggressive and rarely stings

24

Mushrooms

POISONOUS

<u>Caesar's Mushroom</u>

- Found near oaks and pines

POISONOUS

<u>Destroying Angel Mushroom</u>

- Found near edges of woodlands, on lawns, or in grassy meadows near trees or shrubs

A mushroom is not a plant since it cannot produce its own food. It is a fungi that gets its food from decaying vegetation underneath the grass.

POISONOUS

<u>Fairy Ring Mushroom</u>

- Found on lawns after rain

Most wild mushrooms are poisonous. The mushrooms we eat are usually grown in controlled environment grow houses.

Ocean Creatures

Horseshoe Crab

- Actually, it's not a real crab at all. It is more closely related to scorpions, spiders, mites and the extinct trilobite.
- Its blood will gel when it comes into contact with bacteria. Because of this, medical companies use horseshoe crab blood to test for bacteria. They milk some of the blood from the crabs and then return them to the ocean.
- It does not bite or sting.

Fiddler Crab

- Male fiddler crab has one of its front claws much bigger than the other one
- Usually walks sideways because it can walk faster this way than walking forwards
- Makes burrows up to 23 inches deep

Crabs have blue blood because they have copper in it instead of iron like we have.

Blue Crab (Soft Shell Crab)

- If the abdomen is "V" shaped, it is a male. If the abdomen is "U" shaped, it is a female.
- As the crabs grow, a new soft shell forms inside underneath the large hard shell. At this time, they are captured and held in water-filled trays until their outer large hard shell gets loose and is taken off. The crabs are then sold for food as soft shell crabs. Both the shell and crabmeat are eaten.

Female: claw tips are red
Males: claw tips are not red

Ocean Creatures

Moon Jellyfish

- Does not have a brain or any blood
- Eats plankton
- If you get stung, scrape the skin with a credit card to remove the stingers. Then, apply vinegar or saltwater. Do not apply ice since this will help to release more toxin.

POISONOUS

Portuguese Man-O-War

- A beached or dying jellyfish could still sting.
- A sting can cause fever, shock, breathing problems, or a heart attack.

Sand Dollar

- Is a marine animal
- Spines on the underside allow it to creep along the sand
- Mouth is underneath in the middle
- When threatened, baby sand dollars split themselves into two baby sand dollars to increase their population.

Starfish

- Is an animal, not a fish
- Has eye spots, which detect light, at the tip of each of its arms
- Has the ability to regrow its arms if broken
- Tube-like feet on the underside allow it to move around
- Eats clams, oysters, and small fish
- Eaten by sea gulls, sharks, and fish

Ocean Creatures

Dolphin

- Can swim over 18 miles per hour
- Can live 45 to 50 years
- Has been known to come to the aid of an injured dolphin and help it to the surface
- Militaries have used dolphins for various purposes, from finding explosive mines to rescuing lost or trapped humans.

Underside of Stingray

Stingray

- Found in shallow waters
- Floridians are told to shuffle their feet when they go in the ocean. This will scare the stingrays into moving away.
- Ancient Greek dentists used the venom from the stingray's spine to numb the mouth.

Manatee or Sea Cow

- Eats plants and vegetables
- Can live 60 to 70 years
- Native Indians used to grind the bones and then use the powder to treat asthma and earache.
- Commonly found in warm waters, especially near power plants or spring-fed waters. It cannot survive below 60 degrees Fahrenheit.
- Usually has scars due to being hit by boat propellers

Ocean Creatures

Shark

- Usually found in saltwater
- In 2008, 59 unprovoked attacks were recorded worldwide.
- Has been found as deep as one mile below the water surface
- Most sharks need to swim constantly in order to breathe, otherwise, they die. One exception is the nurse shark.
- Some sharks, if they are turned over or stroked on the nose, can become paralyzed for 15 minutes.
- It is believed that sharks do not sleep but may rest parts of their brains for minutes like dolphins do.
- Its skeleton is made of cartilage, not bone. Cartilage is found in the human ear and nose.
- Sharks can see color, similar to humans.

Some sharks lose 30,000 teeth in their lifetime.

Species of sharks include: Blacktip Reef, Bull, Great White, Goblin, Hammerhead, Lemon, Mako, Nurse, Sandtiger, Tiger, Whale, and Zebra sharks.

Parasites

A parasite is an organism that grows, feeds and lives on another animal. The mite, flea and louse all get their food by sucking blood.

Scabies Mite

- Invisible to the human eye
- Burrows under the skin where she lays her eggs
- Causes intense itching and rash

Mite Burrowing Under The Skin In A Straight Path

Flea

- The size of a sesame seed
- Most common is the cat flea
- Causes itching and irritation
- The flea lays her eggs loosely on the cat hair. The eggs then fall on the ground, floor, bedding or furniture where they hatch.
- Heavy infestations are recognized by black specks of undigested blood.

Head Louse

- The size of a sesame seed
- The head louse is the most common in humans.
- Causes itching and irritation
- Lays white eggs called nits that it glues to the hair shaft
- Spread by close contact with an infected person or by using a comb that carries eggs or lice on it.
- Common in young school children

Plants - Flowers

Bird of Paradise

- Can bloom throughout the year
- Closely related to the banana tree

Purple Passion Flower

- Blooms from summer to fall
- Attracts butterflies
- Has medicinal qualities such as inducing sleep

Hydrangea

Slightly POISONOUS

- Blooms in spring
- Acidic soils produce blue flowers and alkaline soils produce pink or purple flowers.

Gardenia

- Blooms from spring to summer
- Sweet smelling
- Belongs to the coffee plant family

Plants - Flowers

Bougainvillea

- Blooms throughout the year
- Named after French admiral and explorer
  Louis Antoine de Bougainville

Crepe Myrtle

- Blooms from spring to summer
- Introduced to the United States
  from China, Korea, and Japan

Hibiscus

- Blooms throughout the year
- Used to make hibiscus tea
  in Africa, Brazil, Cambodia,
  Jamaica, and Mexico
- Poisonous to cats and dogs

Plants - Flowers

Black Eyed Susan

- Blooms from spring to fall
- Attracts butterflies
- American Indians used it to make tea to get rid of colds.

Magnolia

- Blooms from spring to summer
- Pollinated by beetles

Oleander POISONOUS

- Blooms throughout the year
- Poisonous to humans, dogs, and cats
- Contains toxins that affect the heart

Pentas

- Blooms from spring to fall
- Attracts butterflies and hummingbirds

Plants - Fruits

Mango Tree

- Produces fruit late June through December
- Good source of Vitamin C

Orange Tree

- Two varieties are Navel and Valencia. Navel oranges are most abundant from January to March while Valencia oranges are most abundant from May to July.
- Very good source of Vitamin C

Banana Tree

- The leaves grow until a flower emerges which turns into a bunch of bananas. This takes about 10 to 15 months. The trunk then dies but little baby plants surround the base of the trunk. The baby plants will once again grow and produce bananas.
- Very good source of Vitamin B6

Strawberry Plant

- Produces fruit December through April
- Very good source of Vitamin C

Plants - Trees

Pygmy Palm

Sago Palm

The roots of palm trees do not get thicker as they age like other trees do, therefore, they are less likely to cause damage to sidewalks and utilities.

Royal Palm

Queen Palm

Cabbage Palm (Sabel Palmetto)

- Florida's state tree
- Tolerates salt spray and cold very well

Saw Palmetto Palm

- Black bears and white-tailed deer eat the fruit of this palm.
- Its fruit is used in herbal medicines.

Mangrove

- Can obtain fresh water from salt water. Some species block salt at their roots while others secrete the salt through their leaves.

Cypress Tree

- Can live to 1600 years old
- Lives in the wetlands
- Most tolerant of floods

Live Oak Tree

- Can live several hundred years
- Used in the 1800's to build ships

Spanish Moss on Tree

- Also called an air plant because it does not grow roots in soil

Longleaf Pine

- May reach heights of 80 to 100 feet
- 200 years of logging have greatly reduced its numbers

Slash Pine

- Common tree of pine plantations
- Takes 30 years for tree to grow so that it can be used for timber

37

Reptiles - Alligator & Lizards

American Alligator

- Lives 35 to 50 years
- Has a shorter, wider snout whereas the crocodile has a longer, narrower snout
- Weighs about 600 pounds (the same weight as three adult men)
- Hunted for its meat to eat and its skin to make belts, boots, purses, and wallets
- Since the alligator swallows its food whole, it has stones in its stomach to help break up the food.
- The female lays about 35 eggs. If the eggs are turned upside down, the babies will drown.
- If the eggs hatch at 90 to 93 degrees Fahrenheit, they become male.
  If the eggs hatch at 82 to 86 degrees Fahrenheit, they become female.

Green Iguana

- Can live up to 20 years
- When threatened, it will bite, claw, and hit with its tail. If the tailed is grabbed too hard, the iguana will let it break off since it can grow a new one, just like other lizards can.

Reptiles - Lizards

Brown Anole Lizard

- Introduced to Florida from Cuba
- Has a blunt snout whereas the
  Green Anole has a pointy snout
- Does not turn green
- Lives 4 to 8 years

Green Anole Lizard

- Turns brown when stressed
- Has been seen fighting its
  own reflection in a mirror

Lizards eat insects such as grasshoppers, crickets, or spiders.
Their eggs are less than ½ of an inch wide.
Lizards shed their skin as they grow. Then they eat the skin
because it is a good source of calcium and nutrients.

Indo-Pacific Gecko

- Changes color from dark gray
  in the day to very pale at night
- Unlike most lizards, it can make
  squeaking or barking noises.

Five-Lined Skink

- Grows to a length of up to 8 inches
- As the young skink grows, its tail
  changes in color from bright blue to gray.

Reptiles - Snakes

Black Racer
(non-poisonous)

Southern Water Snake
(non-poisonous)

Snake scales are made of keratin, the same material human hair and nails are made of.
While humans have 33 vertebrae which make up our backbone, snakes have 100 to 400 vertebrae.

Corn Snake or Red Rat Snake
(non-poisonous)

Youth Red Rat Snake
(non-poisonous)

Reptiles - Snakes

Yellow Rat Snake
(non-poisonous)

Pueblan Milk Snake
(non-poisonous)

Scarlet Snake
(non-poisonous)

POISONOUS
Eastern Coral Snake

Saying to remember:
Red on yellow kills a fellow;
Red touching black is a friend of Jack.

The Scarlet Snake looks like the Coral Snake
in an attempt to ward off predators.

Reptiles - Snakes

Youth

POISONOUS

Adult

Cottonmouth (Water Moccasin)

- Turns darker in color as it gets older
- Called Cottonmouth because the inside of its mouth is white

Most poisonous snakes have cat shaped pupils instead of round pupils. They also have triangular heads (instead of oval heads) to accommodate their venom glands.

All three of these snakes are pit vipers. Pit vipers use their pit organ (which senses heat) to see their warm blooded prey. The pit organ is a deep pocket located between their eyes and their nose.

POISONOUS
Eastern Diamondback Rattlesnake

- Has the most poisonous venom
- Can cause death

POISONOUS
Pygmy Rattlesnake

- Less than 2 feet long but has a thick body
- Has a distinctive dark line through the eye to the corner of the jaw

The rattle is made of loosely attached, hard, hollow segments. These segments are made of keratin, the same material the scales are made of. When the snake uses its muscles to shake the segments, they hit each other, causing the rattling sound. Each time the snake sheds its skin, a new rattle is formed.

Reptiles - Turtles

Box Turtle

- Males have red eyes and the females have yellowish eyes.
- Can live more than 100 years

Gopher Tortoise

- Spends most of its time digging and living in burrows
- Eats plants

Loggerhead Sea Turtle

- Adult weighs over 250 pounds
- Can swim in the water at 15 miles per hour
- It gets rid of excess salt from the saltwater it drinks through glands located near its tear ducts. That's why sometimes it looks like its crying.
- The female adult returns to the beach where she was born, sometimes even after 30 years.
- Eggs in cooler sands produce more males and eggs in warmer sands produce more females.

The difference between a turtle and a tortoise is that a turtle spends most of its time in the water whereas a tortoise spends its time on land. The tortoise does not have webbed feet for swimming.

A turtle's shell is attached to its body. The inner shell is made of about 60 bones and includes portions of its backbone and ribs. The outer shell is made of keratin. Its shell allows it to retract its head and legs, protecting it from predators. A sea turtle, however, cannot retract its head and flippers. There is no room in the shell because of the big muscles it has for its flippers.

Reptiles - Turtles

The turtle is the only reptile that has no teeth.
It uses its beak to grab and bite food.

Snapping Turtle

- One snap could bite off a finger
- Tail is shaped like a saw

Cooter Turtle

- Can be found basking on logs in the river
- Eats mostly plants but also eats small fish, snails, tadpoles, and insects

The top part of the shell is called the carapace and
the bottom part of the shell is called the plastron.

Red Belly Turtle

- Grows to about 12 inches long
- Sometimes lays its eggs in alligator nests

Soft Shell Turtle

- Has a very long neck
- The shell is actually hard and is covered with leathery skin.

Scorpions & Spiders

Florida Bark Scorpion

- Can reach up to 4 inches long
- Largest of the scorpions in Florida
- The scorpions in Florida are not deadly.
- Its bite hurts more than a wasp bite but medical attention is not required unless a person is allergic to the venom.
- Lives 3 to 5 years
- Glows under ultraviolet light due to the presence of fluorescent chemicals in its exoskeleton

Daddy Long Legs Spider

- Common house spider
- There is an urban myth that this spider has the most poisonous venom. In 2004, however, the "Mythbusters" show proved that the bite from this spider only produced a mild short-lived burning sensation.

This spider is about 1 ½ inches long.

Spiny Orb Weaver Spider

- Not dangerous to humans
- Known for its flat, circular web
- A new web is constructed each night to make sure the web is secure.
- Eats insects

This spider is about ¼ of an inch long.

Spiders

Black Widow Spider

POISONOUS

- Most venomous spider in North America
- Recognizable by the red hourglass on its back
- Only the female bites
- The female may eat the male.
- The bite feels like a pin prick. Fifteen minutes to 1 hour after the bite, symptoms include a dull muscle pain, either in the chest or abdomen. Other symptoms are difficulty breathing, painful muscle cramps, increased sweating, nausea, vomiting, and numbness. The bite rarely causes death.

This spider is about 1½ inches long.

This spider is about 1½ inches long.

Brown Recluse Spider

POISONOUS

- Recognizable by the violin shape on its back
- Unlike most spiders that have 8 eyes, the brown recluse has 6 eyes: one pair in front and one pair on either side.
- Initially, the bite does not hurt but 2 to 8 hours later, symptoms appear. The symptoms include: itching, vomiting, pain, nausea, fever, muscle pain, skin blistering, and possible death of the skin if medical attention is not sought.

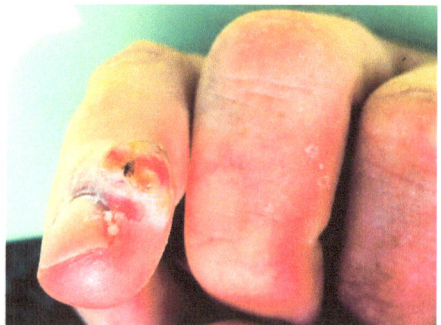

Brown Recluse Bite

Spiders

If you compare an ounce of spider silk and an ounce of steel, spider silk is stronger.

Spider webs contain Vitamin K which helps to clot blood. Hundreds of years ago, webs were used as gauze to stop a wound from bleeding.

Black & Yellow Argiope Spider

- Also known as the writing spider, it is a common garden spider.
- Its bite is not poisonous.
- It is unknown why it makes a zig-zag pattern on its web; perhaps for use as camouflage.

This spider is about 2½ inches long.

Wolf Spider

- Its bite is not poisonous.
- Very common and usually found on the ground. It does not spin webs but hides under debris. It may also dig burrows.

This spider is about 1 inch long.

Snails & Slugs

Snail

- Shell is attached to its body
- If conditions become dry, the snail can pull itself into its shell and secrete a seal over the opening.
- Shell is made of calcium carbonate which is also found in corals, marine animal shells, pearls, starfish, egg shells, limestone, marble, and hard water

Snails are eaten by people in countries all over the world. "Escargot" is a common snail dish served in France.

Slug

- Does not have a shell
- To keep itself moist, it covers itself in mucus that leaves a shiny trail behind as it moves.

Slugs and Snails

- Are active at night, especially after it rains
- Eat plants, fruits, vegetables, dead leaves, and fungus
- Have eyes at the end of their tentacles
- Have a muscular foot that lets them glide along

Index

Index Continued

Acknowledgments

http://plants.ifas.ufl.edu
http://www.marine.usf.edu
http://alligatorfur.com
http://animals.nationalgeographic.com
http://edis.ifas.ufl.edu
http://www.flmnh.ufl.edu
http://www.cas.usf.edu
http://www.springboard4health.com
http://www.coryi.org
http://www.floridabats.org
http://www.kidzone.ws
http://www.ehow.com
http://www.emedicinehealth.com

http://www.wildflorida.com
http://www.sciencedaily.com
http://myfwc.com
http://www.newworldencyclopedia.org
http://www.wikipedia.com
http://www.who.int
http://www.colostate.edu
http://nutritiondata.self.com
http://www.bio.umass.edu
http://www.aa-fishing.com
http://www.britannica.com
http://www.stlwildbirdcenter.com
http://www.nationalzoo.si.edu

Photo Credits

American Cockroach Egg Casing	Department of Entomology, University of Nebraska-Lincoln
American Cockroach Life Stages	Daniel R. Suiter, University of Georgia, Bugwood.org
Black and Yellow Mud Dauber	Howard Ensign Evans, Colorado State University, Bugwood.org
Brown Recluse Spider	Florida Division of Plant Industry Archive, Florida Department of Agriculture and Consumer Services, Bugwood.org
Brown Recluse Spider Bite	Terry S. Price, Georgia Forestry Commission, Bugwood.org
Cloudless Sulphur Caterpillar	Edward L. Manigault, Clemson University, Donated Collection, Bugwood.org
Fall Armyworm	Clemson University - USDA Cooperative Extension Slide Series, Bugwood.org
Fall Armyworm Moth	Lyle Buss, University of Florida, Bugwood.org
Fire Ant Bites	Daniel Wojcik, Bugwood.org
Formosan Subterranean Termite	Scott Bauer, USDA Agricultural Research Service, Bugwood.org
German Cockroach Egg Casing	Department of Entomology, University of Nebraska-Lincoln
Head Lice	Dani Barchana, Self Employed, Bugwood.org
Love Bugs	William M. Johnson, Ph.D., County Extension Agent-Horticulture, Texas AgriLife Extension Service, Galveston County Office
Native Subterranean Termite	Gerald J. Lenhard, Louisiana State University, Bugwood.org
Puss Caterpillar	Lacy L. Hyche, Auburn University, Bugwood.org
Puss Caterpillar Moth	Rebekah D. Wallace, University of Georgia, Bugwood.org
Red Imported Fire Ant	Jake Farnum, Bugwood.org
Saddleback Caterpillar Moth	Lacy L. Hyche, Auburn University, Bugwood.org
Southern Water Snake	Rebekah D. Wallace, University of Georgia, Bugwood.org
Termite Comparison	USDA Forest Service Archive, USDA Forest Service, Bugwood.org
Zebra Longwing Caterpillar	Jerry A. Payne, USDA Agricultural Research Service, Bugwood.org

About The Author

Jacqueline Gonzalez lives in the Tampa Bay area with her young son. She is originally from Winnipeg, Manitoba, Canada where she graduated from University of Manitoba with a Bachelor of Science Honors degree in Geology. After working in the oil industry for a few years, she moved to Florida to work in the environmental geology field. She changed her career after her son was born and opened her own accounting business.

When her son was ten years old, she decided to start writing books that were simple, easy to read, and had a lot of colorful pictures. She believes these are features that would entice both children and adults to read and learn. She plans to continue writing books for her Education for Everyone Series.

www.ingramcontent.com/pod-product-compliance
Lightning Source LLC
Chambersburg PA
CBHW041509280526
45792CB00004B/1188